JOSH DUGGAR

His Drift!

HENDRICH MILLER

Hendrich Miller

Josh Duggar: His Drift

INTRODUCTION

CHAPTER 1

JOSH DUGGAR BIOGRAPHY, NET WORTH

JOSH DUGGAR 19 KIDS AND COUNTING

JOSH DUGGAR CAREER

CHAPTER 2

DISTURBING DETAILS ABOUT JOSH DUGGA

CHAPTER 3

JOSH DUGGAR'S WIFE

CHAPTER 4

DUGGAR FAMILY SCANDAL

CHAPTER 5

19 KIDS AND COUNTING

Josh Duggar: His Drift

INTRODUCTION

Ex-reality star Josh Duggar to be condemned for Child pornography

Previous unscripted television star Josh Duggar will get back to government court on Wednesday, where an adjudicator could condemn him to as long as 20 years in jail for getting and having youngster porn.

Examiners are looking for a most extreme sentence for Duggar, whose huge family was the focal point of TLC's "19 Kids and then some" unscripted TV drama. His legal counsellors have asked the court in Fayetteville, around 140 miles (225 kilometres) northwest of Little Rock, to send him to jail for a very long time.

Duggar was captured in April 2021 after a Little Rock police investigator found youngster pornography records were being shared by a PC followed to Duggar. Specialists affirmed that pictures portraying the sexual maltreatment of youngsters, including babies, were downloaded in 2019 onto a PC at a vehicle sales centre Duggar claimed.

Tender loving care dropped "19 Kids and then some" in 2015 following charges that Duggar had attacked four of his sisters and a sitter years sooner. Specialists began

Josh Duggar: His Drift

investigating the abuse in 2006 after receiving a tip from a family member, but reasoned that the legal deadline for any potential charges had passed.

According to Duggar's family, he admitted to the caressing and apologized. After the claims remerged in 2015, Duggar apologized openly for vague way of behaving and surrendered as a lobbyist for the Family Research Council, a moderate Christian gathering.

Months after the fact, he openly apologized for betraying his significant other and an erotic entertainment fixation, for which he then looked for treatment.

In looking for a 20-year sentence, examiners referred to the realistic pictures - and the periods of the youngsters in question - as well as court declaration about the supposed maltreatment of Duggar's sisters.

Duggar's previous way of behaving "gives a disturbing window into the degree of his sexual interest in kids that the Court ought to consider at condemning," government examiners wrote in their condemning reminder.

"This previous direct, when seen close by the lead for which he has been sentenced, clarifies that Duggar has a firmly established, unavoidable, and vicious sexual interest in kids, and a readiness to follow up on that interest" the court documenting said.

"No sign that Duggar will at any point make the strides important to change this example of conduct"

Examiners additionally noticed that Duggar's PC had been apportioned to avoid responsibility programming that had been introduced to answer to his significant other action, for example, pornography look, subject matter authorities agree.

"There is only no sign that Duggar will anytime take the steps critical to change this illustration of lead and address his tendency for minor females," analysts made.

Duggar has kept up with that he's guiltless and that he plans to pursue, his lawyers wrote in their condemning reminder.

Judge Rules Against New Trial Day Before Sentencing, Says 'Contention Lacks Merit'

Josh Duggar's preliminary finished in December 2021 with a blameworthy decision on two counts of getting and having youngster sexual maltreatment material. Presently, his condemning date draws near. On May 25, 2022, the adjudicator will sentence Josh for his

Josh Duggar: His Drift

violations. Furthermore, his lawful group's new endeavour to achieve another preliminary before his condemning was recently denied. Here is the most recent Josh Duggar news.

Late Josh Duggar news is tied in with condemning — and everything continuing lawfully before it works out. As indicated by 40/29 News, Josh's lawyers mentioned another preliminary preceding condemning. Their solicitation was denied on Tuesday, May 24, 2022. The report noticed the lawyers asserted there wasn't sufficient proof to convict Josh, and they additionally guaranteed examiners didn't uncover proof rapidly enough. However, Judge Timothy L Brooks denied this.

"His contention is that no sensible jury might have found he intentionally got and had kid erotic entertainment since there is deficient proof that he, or any other person besides, saw the pictures," the archives read. "Mr. Duggar's contention needs merit, as there is more than adequate proof, he saw the pictures of kid sexual entertainment that had been downloaded to his business PC.

The records then delve into additional subtleties and a summation of what happened at the preliminary.

The new Josh Duggar news with respect to the refusal of another preliminary means condemning will, for sure, occur on May 25, 2022. Anyway, what time will Josh Duggar be condemned?

Condemning happens at 9:30 a.m. CT on Wednesday, May 25, 2022, in Arkansas.

The indictment trusts Josh will get 20 years in the slammer; however, his lawful group expects a lighter sentence. A condemning update from the indictment expresses there's "no sign" that Josh will do whatever it may take to "change this example of conduct and address his preference for minor females

The arraignment likewise called Josh "a guilty party who has a background marked by physically mishandling minors, who has not gotten any treatment or treatment for this direct to discuss, who seems improbable to at any point search out or genuinely take part in treatment or treatment to address this lead, and who keeps on rejecting any obligation for his past or present wrongdoings."

The Duggar family stays calm in front of condemning

With condemning approaching, how does the Duggar family feel? Jim Bob and Michelle Duggar haven't

Josh Duggar: His Drift

expressed much since December 2021, and they keep their virtual entertainment posts restricted. Josh Duggar's significant other, Anna Duggar, additionally hasn't posted a lot of via online entertainment. However she included a connection her Instagram page that proposes she has faith in her significant other's honesty.

Moreover, Anna composed a letter to the appointed authority in front of condemning. The letter subtleties how she accepts Josh ought to be home with his family, as he gives and helps with bringing up their seven children. Michelle likewise composed a letter lauding Josh's great-hearted nature.

Hendrich Miller

Josh Duggar: His Drift

CHAPTER 1

Josh Duggar Biography, Net worth

Joshua James Duggar (Josh Duggar) is an American TV character, political dissident and previously utilized vehicle sales rep. He was brought into the world on March third, 1988 in Tontitown, Washington DC.

His folks are James Robert and Michelle Annette Ruark Duggar. He was raised in a moderate Christian home. He self-taught and passed yet he didn't attend a university. He is broadly known for his appearances on the unscripted TV drama, 19 Kids and then some. Duggar was the Executive Director of FRC activity which was a Lobbying PAC supported by the Family Research Council as from June 2013 to May 2015.

After it was found that Duggar had attacked five young ladies somewhere in the range of 2002 and 2003 and had been an individual from the site Ashley Madison prompted the wiping out of 19 Kids and Counting back on July 16, 2015. His outrage was named among the main 10 embarrassments of 2015 by USA Today while the Washington Post recorded Duggar as one of the "15 People the Internet Hated Most in 2015".

Josh Duggar: His Drift

He was born on 3rd March, 1988 in Tontitown, Washington DC. He is 30 years old beginning around 2018.

Josh And Anna Duggar| Josh Duggar Wife

Josh has been hitched to Anna Duggar since September 26th, 2008. They have five youngsters.

He has 5 youngsters; Michael James Duggar, Mackynzie Renée Duggar, Marcus Anthony Duggar, Mason Garett Duggar, and Meredith Grace Duggar.

Coming up next are his kin; Jana Duggar, John-David Duggar, Jill Duggar Dillard, Jessa Duggar, Jinger Duggar, Joseph Duggar, Josiah Duggar, Joy-Anna Duggar, Jedidiah Duggar, Jeremiah Duggar, Jason Duggar, James Duggar, Justin Duggar, Jackson Duggar, Johannah Duggar, Jennifer Duggar, Jordyn-Grace Makiya Duggar and Josie Duggar.

On August nineteenth, 2015, a group which had been exploring Josh distributed a story declaring that he had kept a paid record on AshleyMadison.com while he was working for the Family Research Council.

A record with a Mastercard that had a place with Joshua J. Duggar, whose charging address matched a home claimed by Mary Duggar in Fayetteville, AR, paid a sum of $986.76 for two separate Ashley Madison memberships between February 2013, and May 2015.

Josh gave the accompanying rundown of turn-ons that he was searching for:

proficient/very much prepped, smart/tasteful, relaxed pants/shirt type, solid/fit body, dainty figure, tall level, short level, long hair, short hair, young lady nearby, devious young lady, funny bone, creative mind, innovative and courageous, loose and agreeable, forceful/assume responsibility nature, certainty, caution/mystery, great audience, great individual cleanliness, normal sex drive, high sex drive, loathes schedule, has a mystery love home, infection free, drug free, regular bosoms

The subsequent record, which was opened in July of 2014, was connected to his home in Oxon Hill, Maryland. The main record utilized a birthday one month before his genuine birthday, while the subsequent one utilized a birthday one day prior. At the point when the subsequent record was opened, he paid a $250 expense that has all the earmarks of being for an "issue ensure".

Josh Duggar: His Drift

Josh Duggar 19 Kids and Counting

19 Kids and then some (previously 17 Kids and then some and 18 Kids and then some) is an American unscripted tv show that broadcasted on the link channel TLC for quite a long time until it's wiping out in 2015. The show includes the Duggar family: guardians Jim Bob and Michelle Duggar and their 19 kids — 9 young ladies and 10 young men, every one of whose names start with the letter "J". During the existence of the show, three kids were conceived, three youngsters were hitched, and four grandkids were conceived. The show was anyway dropped after an outrage including Josh surfaced.

Josh Duggar Career

Duggar appeared on TLC as a significant part of reality program, 19 Kids and then some. Starting in 2005, he appeared on before shows about his family on Discovery Health, when Duggar was 17 years old. The wedding of Josh Duggar and Anna Keller was featured in a show scene named A Very Duggar Wedding circulating on January 25, 2009.

It consolidated the wedding orchestrating, status, practice, capacity and get-together. Duggar and his soul mate have communicated they saved their most memorable kiss for their important day. Different scenes report Duggar's youths including GrandDuggar's First Birthday circulating December 7, 2010, where Duggar compliments his daughter Mackynzie's most memorable birthday festivity and proclaims the typical birth of their ensuing kid; First Grandson, broadcasting June 19, 2011, featured Duggar and his soul mate introducing their resulting kid, Michael James; and GrandDuggar Makes 3! broadcasting June 16, 2013, a Father's Day unprecedented introducing the Duggars' third new-born child, Marcus Anthony.

A remarkable named Josh and Anna: Our Story broadcast on October 22, 2013, which reviewed the couple's underlying five years of marriage. Duggar and his significant other proclaimed the ordinary birth of their fourth youth on a scene named Anna's Having A... , which revealed May 12, 2015. The scene consolidated the Duggars announcing the ultrasound showed they were having another young woman.

Exactly when Duggar was a juvenile, his father, Jim Bob Duggar, was a two-term Republican person from the Arkansas House of Representatives. Duggar has in like manner been dynamic in preservationist legislative

Josh Duggar: His Drift

issues; while running a vehicle merchant he worked as low upkeep political counsellor in 2007 under the business name Strategic Political Services.

In 2008, he worked on the Republican official fundamental campaign of past Arkansas Governor Mike Huckabee. In 2012, Joshua Duggar would in general prepare for the Republican official contender Rick Santorum of Pennsylvania.

From June 2013 to May 2015, he was true head of FRC Action, a political movement and battling affiliation upheld by the Family Research Council. While portraying what is happening with the affiliation, he communicated that he would be based on "attracting the grassroots and taking the message of certainty, family and opportunity the entire way across America".

Family Research Council president Tony Perkins expressed that by contracting Duggar they would have jumped at the chance to address dynamically young people by making the most of the commonness of the Duggar family TV course of action. He further imparted, "The colossal piece of Josh's centre will collect our grass-roots the nation over".

While working at FRC Action, preservationist Republican candidates regarded Duggar as a way to deal with impel their messages to his constituents. He fought for Republican Senate candidates in Kansas, Mississippi, and Virginia before the 2014 midterm races.

He portrayed his family as the "epitome of preservationist regards" and sponsor for what he terms "family-centred" and conservative Christian right political points of view, including protection from embryo expulsion, detachment, and gay marriage. Joshua Duggar has been implied as a "unfriendly to gay lobbyist" by GLAAD, a pro LGBT freedoms affiliation once in the past known as the Gay and Lesbian Alliance Against Defamation.

Josh Duggar: His Drift

CHAPTER 2

DISTURBING DETAILS ABOUT JOSH DUGGA

Court reports uncover that Josh had 65 express pictures of young ladies between the ages of seven and nine years of age. He likewise had recordings of youngsters a similar age.

"An ensuing legal assessment of that gadget and different gadgets seized from the respondent and the vehicle parcel compliant with the warrant uncovered proof showing that the litigant utilized the HP Desktop to download from the web and, hence, have various records portraying minors participated in physically express direct," the public authority's short peruses.

On Reddit, Duggar family devotees are examining these new subtleties. One client expresses, "I feel like it's basically impossible that Anna really knows the subtleties. This article most likely contains much more data than she (and the remainder of the family, with the exception of perhaps JB) know. Not that I wish injury on anybody, however I wish they all needed to peruse the subtleties and comprehend what he did."

Josh Duggar: His Drift

Since Josh's capture, there have been many inquiries regarding what the family really is familiar with his supposed violations. A few clients think Jim Bob, Michelle, and Anna ought to be in the court during the preliminary. They feel that they must get familiar with the seriousness of the case.

In spite of the proof against Josh, his significant other Anna apparently still trusts he's guiltless. Sources say she's investing a great deal of energy at his gatekeepers' home. Furthermore, she even carries the children with her to visit her significant other.

Caution: a portion of the subtleties from the court recording in this story are realistic.

Making a course for his preliminary for supposedly having and getting youngster porn, previous "19 Kids and then some" unscripted television star Josh Duggar has requested that a government judge request investigators to turn over data about the specialists who purportedly busted him.

Government examiners went against that bid on Monday as an "impermissible fishing trip for proof that is either non-existent, unimportant to his safeguard, or currently created," in another legitimate brief that reveals insight into the beginnings of the examination.

The recording answers a movement to constrain data documented by Duggar's lawyer Justin Gelfand in late July, which zeroed in vigorously on Little Rock Detective Amber Kalmer.

"This Case is Straightforward"

Duggar's protection group guarantees that two other cops in Arkansas likewise downloaded the records, and they believe the public authority should deliver data about them.

For the investigators, the secret officials are an interruption.

"In spite of the litigant's rehashed chant, the two officials were not associated with the United States' government examination of the respondent and they didn't give the arraignment group any materials," Assistant U.S. Lawyer Dustin Roberts wrote in a 14-page legitimate brief. "They surely were not following up for the United States concerning this case, as made sense of in more detail above, and the litigant's solicitation for this supposed Brady material ought to hence be denied."

Josh Duggar: His Drift

Examiners counter that those officials assumed no part in the public authority's examination, and they say that Duggar's legitimate group is unnecessarily convoluting the situation.

"Likewise with many cases in view of secret examinations of people sharing kid sexual maltreatment material ("CSAM") over distributed networks, this case is direct," the short states

As indicated by the indictment, the case's starting points follow over quite a while back, with a criminal investigator utilizing "BitTorrent programming intended for policing" find the exchange of life as a youngster sexual maltreatment material that would ultimately be connected to a high-profile target.

On May 14, 2019, Detective Kalmar downloaded documents over the BitTorrent shared network, which she said she followed to an IP address in Northwest Arkansas.

The analyst says that she sent the lead to Homeland Security Investigations Agent Gerald Faulkner, who said the web trail drove him to Duggar's little pre-owned vehicle showroom in Arkansas: Wholesale Motorcars. Faulkner says he utilized the tip to lay out reasonable justification on the side of a warrant on Duggar's showroom.

"Different Files Depicting Minors"

In a testimony revealed on Monday, Faulkner says that the records specialists followed to Duggar's IP address in May 2019 were a ".zip" organizer and one more as a video, and both supposedly portrayed juvenile young ladies between the ages of seven and nine being physically manhandled.

The initial, a compress record, contained 65 picture documents of one little kid of that age "lying on her back and utilizing her hands to uncover her vagina and butt," the oath states.

The second, specialists say, showed two juvenile young ladies "both totally exposed laying on top of one another."

"A male subject is then seen infiltrating one of the juvenile female's vagina with his erect penis," the testimony states.

As uncovered at Duggar's detainment hearing in May, Agent Faulkner got the pursued warrant on Nov. 4, 2019.

Josh Duggar: His Drift

Exactly four days after the fact, Faulkner executed the hunt and found more pictures and recordings showing adolescence sexual maltreatment on gadgets in the unscripted television star's showroom.

"A following criminological evaluation of that device and various contraptions seized from the defendant and the vehicle part according to the warrant uncovered proof appearance that the respondent used the HP Desktop to download from the web and, along these lines, have different records depicting minors partook in truly unequivocal lead," the public power's latest brief summarizes.

During the May hearing, Agent Faulkner called one famous record, named "Daisy's Destruction," among the "Best Five most terrible of just horrible" he at any point needed to inspect, as it portrayed the maltreatment of a 18-month old little child. The one who made the record, sentenced Australian human dealer Peter Scully, is carrying out a daily existence punishment in the Philippines.

Hendrich Miller

Josh Duggar: His Drift

CHAPTER 3

Josh Duggar's Wife

Anna Duggar was once generally famous for her appearances on the TLC show, 19 Kids to say the least, which followed her better half's family as they investigated life as an incredibly gigantic self-showing Christian family.

What Is Anna Duggar's Net Worth?

Anna Duggar

Anna Duggar was once generally well known for her appearances on the TLC show, 19 Kids to say the least, which followed her significant other's family as they investigated life as an especially gigantic self-showing Christian family.

Her name has actually become indivisible from her soul mate's name due to his sexual abuse case.

All through the various shames and lawful questions that have arisen, she not altogether settled to stay devoted to her better half and backing him through the most troublesome part of his life.

Josh Duggar: His Drift

Anna Duggar has an all-out resource of $50,000, which she secured through her experience on 19 Kids and Endlessly depending On before TLC dropped the series completely.

Regardless, her all out resources could lessen rapidly accepting her better half is considered accountable close by the potential censuring.

Duggar was brought into the world in South Florida on June 23rd of 1988 to Suzette Keller and Michael E. Keller, with whom she was for each situation exceptionally close.

Once each week, the Keller family would have 15-minute social events with their people to inspect how their lives were going and the fights they were at present facing.

Like her soul mate, Anna Duggar experienced youth in a gigantic family, being the fifth of the Keller's' eight young people.

She has four sisters and three kin.

Growing up the posterity of a prison minister, they were raised with serious Christian characteristics and were told by their people.

This inferred that the children expected to demand that assent under the watchful eye of picking court someone and could date someone accepting they wanted to marry them.

Ensuing to meeting Josh Duggar at a self-showing gathering, she imparted her love for him to her mother before the families made game arrangements for the two youngsters to date.

When seeing somebody, number of concludes that ought to have been followed extended.

The standards at first set up turned out to be trying while at the same time pondering what ended up joking around Duggar who is faulted for sexual abuse.

The financial fights that few has looked since Duggar was revealed have obliged them to sell their family home that they had actually updated and move back in with different family members.

Appearing On 19 Kids and Counting

Anna Duggar appeared in an impressive part of the episodes of 19 Kids to say the least, starting in 2008 with the episode Josh Gets Engaged.

Josh Duggar: His Drift

The group was truly prepared to see their recommendation because of a mysterious camera that was set up at Gator Landing, the restaurant where Anna was eating with her people when Josh Duggar stunned her and proposed.

The accompanying episode that Anna Duggar expected an immense part in was Duggar Dating Rules.

During this episode, watchers would find that the Duggar kids are not allowed to contact their perfect partners until they're secured, ought to save their most vital kiss for their wedding, and are never allowed to be isolated from every other person with their soul mates until they're hitched.

During the episode Once a Bride, always a Duggar, watchers got an inside look at the readiness of Anna and Josh Duggar's wedding.

The Duggar family feels that they ought to do everything together, especially with respect to the readiness of a celebratory event like a wedding.

Their wedding was moreover a transmission event, being featured on the 2009 episode A Very Duggar Wedding.

Disorder follows as the Duggar watchmen battle the rest of the Duggar family together for the wedding.

Around a similar time, Anna Duggar and her soul mate moved out of his family's home and moved into their generally noteworthy home.

New Duggars on the Block walked watchers through them as of late purchased home and the moving framework.

Before the presentation of Anna Duggar's most critical youngster, Michelle Duggar took her young lady in-guideline out to go exchange shopping and took her actual tests for the kid in the episode Duggars at the Doctors.

After Anna Duggar had her daughter, the family broadcast the Duggar kinfolk meeting the family's most critical grandchild in the episode First GrandDuggar.

She would appear in significantly more episodes until the show's end in 2015.

After 19 Kids and Counting was dropped, TLC endeavoured to bring a part of the Duggars back for their own show called Counting On in 2015.

Josh Duggar: His Drift

Out of the 119 episodes that ran from 2015 until 2021, Anna Duggar showed up in 40 of them.

The primary episode of Counting On that Anna Duggar appeared in was A New Chapter, where sisters Jill and Jessa examine what is the deal with their most settled kin and how his exercises have affected them all through the long haul.

While Anna Duggar and her children were energetically allowed to be on the show, her soul mate was disallowed from the show over his assault cases.

He is one of just a modest bunch of excellent people from the family that you don't see on Counting On, a move that devotees of the family and show were happy to see.

In the episode Counting One More, Jessa and her better half Ben centre around going through the gathering cycle while having a spot with a family that has little to no faith in there of brain to their certainty.

During the episode, Anna Duggar gives her sister-in-law her full assistance and expectations all that turns out for her of karma through the cycle.

The last episode that Anna Duggar shows up in for the show is A New Life

Regardless of the way that season 12 was organized, nobody knows what will happen to Counting On.

It is foggy at this point if we'll be seeing the Duggars in their organization show anytime sooner rather than later or anytime later on.

Getting Her Education to Home-school Her Children

Anna Duggar has reliably grown up around families that have self-trained their adolescents, and she knew starting from the starting that she expected to do similarly

While encountering adolescence in the certainty of her family, she was bestowed with the meaning of getting hitched, having children, and bringing them up in comparable certainty she and her family were raised in.

To turn into the best mother, she and her sisters went through an online Christian school program in youth headway.

While Anna Duggar has never demonstrated the kind of degree she gained from this program, most have

Josh Duggar: His Drift

acknowledged that it was either an undergrad program or an Associate's Degree

Especially like her own mother and her mother in law, Anna Duggar not altogether firmly established to self-show all of the seven of her own youths.

Concerning self-instructing, she triumphs ultimately each and every piece of her proposal from her mother, mother-in-law, and various mothers who are veterans of self-educating.

Despite the way that her children are still incredibly energetic, Duggar regularly goes to the watchmen of additional carefully prepared youths who are fundamental for a comparable certainty as the Duggars.

She acknowledges that the mothers of young people have more understanding and can recall make ideas about what they did well for sure they would have done differently.

Anna Duggar acknowledges that self-showing her children gives them additional holding time that watchmen lose while sending their youths to government supported school

Under the careful focus of the legitimate debates against her soul mate, Duggar would routinely post by means of virtual amusement about the enjoyments of self-instructing.

These days, Anna Duggar has quieted through internet-based amusement, simply introducing on report the presentation of her seventh young person.

Considering all that she and her family are going through, it's smart that she would get away from online diversion.

Her Husband's Sexual Abuse Case

The sexual abuse group of proof against Anna Duggar's better half may simply have shown up at the public's eye lately, but Josh Duggar has had police contentions reported against him since March of 2002.

The fundamental person to report his exercises to the police was his father.

Jim Bob Duggar went to the police after he investigated his youngster.

In the 33-page report, around four or five episodes were represented.

Josh Duggar: His Drift

In May of 2002, Jim Bob Duggar ran as a Republican competitor to address Arkansas in the United States Senate.

His central goal focused in on reprimanding attack and inbreeding, communicating that they should be seen as capital bad behaviours and repelled to the furthest level of the law

The Cheating Scandal

Anna Duggar has reliably complied with the rules of having the kind of relationship she was ensured, yet clearly Josh Duggar has not had comparative steadfastness to these standards or their marriage

In 2015, Josh Duggar was one of thousands of misdirecting life accomplices who were outed when developers set all the client information liberated from Ashley Madison.

Ashley Madison was a web-based help that allowed married men to find women with whom they would unobtrusively and deliberately deceive their mates.

In spite of transparently showing up as customary a relationship as could genuinely be expected, Duggar had added a hazardous idea to his web-based data.

This included looking for just easy-going hook-ups and interests in investigating various roads with respect to sexual stuff.

The developer had revealed that Josh Duggar had two records on the infamous untrustworthiness site and had consumed $986.76 on the site.

Clients of the site would be offered limits if they didn't have an unsanctioned sentiment in somewhere near 90 days of their obtaining of $250 or more.

To ensure that the charging wasn't connected to him in any way, Josh Duggar used his

Josh Duggar: His Drift

CHAPTER 4

Duggar family Scandal

Attack allegations against previous "19 Kids and then some" reality star Josh Duggar prompted the show's wiping out after 15 seasons.

In May 2015, it was uncovered that a police report from 2006 showed Duggar had been investigated for evidently going after five underage young women.

His folks, Jim Bob and Michelle Duggar, later told Fox News that Duggar had attacked four of their little girls and a sitter.

The disclosures drove the unscripted TV drama's organization TLC to drop the show.

"I acted unpardonably for which I am very grieved and profoundly lament. I hurt others, including my family and dear companions," Josh Duggar said in an explanation at that point.

##It took Jim Bob Duggar over a year to report his child's activities to the specialists, as per a police report.

A 2006 police report got by In Touch magazine in 2015 demonstrated that Jim Bob originally became mindful of

Josh Duggar: His Drift

allegations against his child in 2002, and further allegations were made in 2003.

In 2003, Jim Bob informed senior his relatives' congregation, the report said, and they concurred the then-teen ought to be shipped off a Christian treatment program. Likewise, that year, as indicated by the report, Jim Bob took his child to see a state officer, and Josh let him know what had occurred. The state officer gave him a "harsh talk," as indicated by the report, however didn't take matters further. (He has since communicated regret.

The charges were simply spread the word for experts in 2006 after a family companion composed a letter enumerating Josh Duggar's activities.

"That letter had been set in a book and had subsequently been ignored. Actually [in 2006] the book had been progressed to someone else with the letter in it and another person tracked down the letter," the Duggars told police.

A source messaged the Oprah show before the family's appearance in 2006 itemizing the claims of attack. Harpo Studios, who ran the Oprah Winfrey Show, then, at that point, faxed the letter to the Department of Human Services hotline, who opened an examination.

Police didn't seek after charges in light of the fact that, at that point, the legal time limit was three years, and it had lapsed.

Josh Duggar was likewise engaged with an embarrassment subsequent to being uncovered as a client on the famous tricking site Ashley Madison.

Josh Duggar was a client somewhere in the range of 2012 and 2015. Duggar, a Christian, had hitched his significant other, Anna, in 2008, and at the hour of the Ashley Madison disclosure in 2015, they had four youngsters together.

He owned up to the cases and put out an announcement, referring to himself as "the greatest fraud of all time."

"While maintaining certainty and family values, I have quickly all through late years been seeing sexual diversion on the web and this transformed into a strange oppression and I became fickle to my soul mate," Duggar said.

Josh Duggar: His Drift

He and his better half stay together, and she is anticipating their seventh youngster

In April, he was accused of ownership of youngster sexual entertainment.

On April 29, 2021, Duggar was captured and held in prison in Washington County, Arkansas. It was uncovered the next day that Duggar had argued not blameworthy to getting and having kid erotic entertainment.

A government specialist affirmed on May 5 that Duggar downloaded and had 65 pictures of youngster sexual entertainment, Insider detailed.

An appointed authority requested Duggar's delivery from prison, and he was delivered on bond on May 6. He wasn't permitted to get back and will rather remain with two companions as he sits tight for his preliminary. Whenever sentenced, he faces as long as 20 years in jail and fines of up to $250,000.

Following his capture, the Duggar family answered the charges, saying, "We value your proceeded with petitions for our family right now. The allegations brought against Joshua today are intense. It is our request that reality, regardless it is, will become known, and that this will be generally settled promptly."

Jill Duggar's significant other, Derick Dillard, posted homophobic and transphobic tweets.

In 2017, Dillard offered slandering remarks about individual TLC reality star and transsexual lobbyist Jazz Jennings. As per People, Dillard referred to Jennings' show as "I'm Jazz" "a paradoxical expression" for being a "unscripted TV drama which follows a non-reality." He likewise called being transsexual "a fantasy" and said that "Orientation isn't liquid; it's appointed by God."

Dillard later said on Twitter that he accepted Jazz was being "exploited, as a feature of a bigger plan," however he over and over misgendered her all the while.

Following his remarks, TLC said something reporting Dillard would never again be showing up on the organization, including Jill Duggar's side project show, "Depending On."

"We need to tell our watchers that Derick Dillard has not taken part in that frame of mind for a really long time and the organization has no designs to highlight him later on," the organization said. "We need to emphasize that Derick's own assertions don't mirror the perspectives on the organization. Attention is pleased to share the tale of Jazz Jennings and her family and will keep on doing as such."

Then in May 2018, TLC tweeted around one of its shows, "Nate and Jeremiah by Design," which featured Nate Berkus, spouse Jeremiah Brent, and their two youngsters.

"What a misfortune of family," Dillard composed due to TLC's tweet. "It's hopeless the manner by which prominent the liberal arrangement is, so much that it the two elements and lauds a lifestyle so defiling to youths on open TV like it should be ordinary

In the wake of getting reaction for the tweet, the dad of-two shielded his remarks, saying, "They influence this unfortunate kid, as well as what depravities are praised. On the off chance that it was infidelity, I question an organization would rush to zero in on the truth of maybe it was alright."

"I'm not slamming individuals, I'm simply getting down on the public plan at play and how an organization picks what they feature," he proceeded.

The Duggar family's live-in coach wedded a man who had whenever been sentenced for rape.

In 2017, it was accounted for that the Duggar family's live-in guide, Tabitha Paine, was locked in to Timothy Robertson, a family companion. In any case, the news before long turned into an embarrassment when it arose that Robertson had been accused of rape in 1999.

As per In Touch, Robertson confessed to criminal sexual direct in an exhaustive round of questioning and gotten a three-year jail sentence. Nonetheless, the sentence was suspended by the appointed authority engaged with the case. Robertson was put waiting on the post-trial process for one year and was requested to pay $943 in compensation.

Robertson was additionally put on the sex wrongdoer library yet was taken off in 2008 when he was exonerated for his wrongdoing by the South Carolina Board of Probation, Parole, and Pardon Services

He later asserted that he was dishonestly blamed for carrying out the wrongdoing, in spite of the fact that he had confessed.

As per the Daily Mail, the Duggars set up a commitment party for the couple, and Tabitha Paine and Timothy Robertson have been hitched for a very long time.

Josh Duggar: His Drift

Hendrich Miller

CHAPTER 5
19 kids and counting

If you haven't heard of the massive (and growing) Duggar Family, then you might be a pop culture novice. This giant family was the star of one of TLC's most popular shows of all time: 19 Kids and Counting, from 2008 to 2015. Dad, Jim Bob Duggar, and his long-time wife, Michelle Duggar, are members of an ultra-religious and politically conservative community that values modesty, obeying the patriarch as head of a family, and above all else, having lots and lots of children. The family has been widely questioned in the media for their anti-gay, conservative "values voter" views.

But even before their many family scandals became public, millions of viewers tuned in every week to see the inner workings of their super-sized family life. Popular episodes have included details about how in the world the Duggars manage to do laundry, dishes, and cook for that many people. And what about bathroom privacy (answer: they have nine bathrooms and seven showers in their 7000 square foot house). Want to know more about Jim Bob, Michelle, Joshua, Jana, John-David, Jill, Jessa, Jinger, Joseph, Josiah, Joy-Anna, Jedidiah, Jeremiah, Jason, James, Justin, Jackson, Johannah,

Jennifer, Jordyn-Grace and Josie? Follow along if you're intrigued, and we'll give you the rundown on the untold truth of 19 Kids and Counting.

The family and show were rocked by sex abuse scandal

In May, 2015 in Touch broke the story that the eldest boy from the 19 Kids and Counting clan Joshua Duggar, had been investigated for (and admitted to) molesting five underage girls when he was a teenager. More than one of the girls were reportedly his sisters. In Touch was able to access a hidden police report from 2006 via a Freedom of Information Act request that detailed the incidents, including police interviews with the two parents, but not with Josh himself. The abuses would likely never have come to light if, according to interviews, a family friend who was in the know hadn't written notes about Josh's actions, stashed them in a book, and then forgetfully lent the book to a friend who discovered the letter and notified police in 2006 (you can't make this stuff up).

The family and certain members of their religious community knew about the attacks that occurred from 2002-2003, but did not immediately alert authorities. The report notes that rather than be tried by law enforcement, Jim Bob instead "met with the elders of

Josh Duggar: His Drift

[his] church and told them what was going on." Josh was reportedly sent to a "Christian Program" where he would supposedly undergo "hard physical work and counselling." However, as was also uncovered in the police reports, Michelle Duggar later admitted to police that he had merely been sent to stay with a family friend to help him with his construction business.

The documents also revealed that Jim Bob blocked police requests to interview Josh. Although the investigation had to be abandoned due to the statute of limitations, Josh, the Duggar family, and TLC became the focus of a media frenzy. Josh and his family were widely criticized for the circumstances of the crimes, their handling of the crimes, and their perceived hypocrisy in the face of their extensive and controversial "family values activism."

The show was cancelled during its highest rated season

Amid all the pressure coming from the public and from other media outlets, in July 2015, TLC announced that it would no longer air 19 Kids and Counting. In their press release statement, the network stated they were "especially concerned for the victims in this situation, including the Duggar family."

In light of criticism that the network continued to air new episodes of 19 Kids and Counting for over a year after the scandal was unearthed, and was seemingly using the molestation case as a ratings booster, TLC worked with "victims' rights and advocacy organizations" to produce a 60 minute documentary about victims of abuse. However, since this documentary also starred the Duggars, it did little to squelch negative public judgement.

Josh had a porn addiction and a secret account on an "infidelity" website

In another shocking development a few weeks later, Gawker, the former flagship publication of heavy-hitter Gawker Media, broke the story that in a massive hack of AshleyMadison.com, the notorious extramarital affair hook-up website, Josh Duggar's name and address was publicly associated with two separate monthly "affair guaranteed" level accounts, for which he had so far paid "a total of $986.76." Josh, who had proposed to his wife on an episode of 19 Kids and Counting, remained mum for a few weeks, and then posted a public apology on his mother Michelle's popular blog.

His apology included the following statement: "While espousing faith and family values, I have secretly over the last several years been viewing pornography on the internet and this became a secret addiction and I became unfaithful to my wife."

The kids are home schooled with an... interesting curriculum

Get ready to a) get some insight into the questionable reason the Duggar parents treated Josh's molestation crimes the way they did and b) feel extremely creeped out. It's common knowledge that the Duggars have long chosen to home school their kids. But did you know that the Christian curriculum they follow has its own share of sexual abuse scandals?

Gawker (which we're pretty sure is the Duggars' least favourite publication) reported in 2015 that the family adheres to a home-schooling program from the Advanced Training Institute, which is "a Bible-based home-schooling program run by alleged cult figurehead Bill Gotthard." Gotthard himself has been accused of a slew of improper sexual advances on young girls, but that's not where the creepiness ends. The curriculum itself has an entire section on what to do when an older male child sexually abuses a younger child of the same family (!).

Another Gawker article reported on one such "lesson," which guides parents on what to do if they discover that "an older brother was guilty of sexually abusing younger ones in his family." When the older brother had "repented," he's asked a series of questions — including "What teaching could have been given to each child [emphasis ours] to resist evil?" and "What factors in the home contributed to immodesty and temptation?" The similarities are eerie, no?

They have been associated with the controversial Quiver full movement

While the belief system of the 19 Kids and Counting family appears to match up exactly with the controversial "Quiver full" movement of Christianity, which has ties with the Duggars' ministry, the family has stated that they do not consider themselves as part of that group. The Quiver full name comes from Psalm 127 which compares one's children to an archer's quiver full of arrows. The extremely conservative and religious group believes it's a woman's duty to produce as many children as possible while in their childbearing years. Nancy Campbell, a representative of the Quiver full movement has publicly stated the group's belief that they are building an army for God. In a blog post on her site Above Rubies, she called a fruitful womb a "weapon against Satan."

Jim Bob once served in the House of Representatives

Long before 19 Kids and Counting, as well as the scandal, the fame, and the money that comes along with being the star of a hit reality TV series, family patriarch, Jim Bob Duggar served his state of Arkansas as a House Representative. He ran on an anti-abortion, family values platform, and served for one term in the early 2000s, before challenging the Arkansas incumbent for his senate seat and losing in 2002.

Josh has been called an "anti-gay activist"

A few years before any news of his sex scandals reached the public, Josh Duggar openly accepted a position with "anti-gay rights" group, the Family Research Council. The FRC has been "classified as an anti-gay hate group by the Southern Poverty Law Centre, and has a long history of attacking the LGBT community and their friends, family and allies."

Hendrich Miller

CHAPTER 6

Josh Duggar Sentencing Date

Disgraced past reality star Josh Duggar will acknowledge what his future holds when he faces censuring on May 25 in the Western District of Arkansas Federal Court on two charges of getting and having young person pornography. The denouncing hearing will happen at 9:30 a.m. neighbourhood time (CST).

When Was Josh Duggar Found Guilty?

A jury saw the most seasoned Duggar kid to be entirely liable of the two-youth pornography relies upon December 9, 2021, following a six-day starter.

How Long Has Josh Duggar Been in Custody?

Duggar has been in power starting there ahead and saved in confinement for his own security.

What Is the Maximum Sentence Josh Duggar Could Receive?

He faces as long as 20 years in jail on each consolidate and up to $250,000 in fines when he is impugned, and his authentic advisors and relatives have been battling the designated master for mercy.

What Sentence Is the Prosecution Asking for?

Duggar's insurance legal counsellors recorded a denouncing update with the court on May 11, mentioning a merged prison sentence of five years. The arraignment is asking that the past 19 Kids and Counting star serve the restriction of 20 years in prison for each count independently.

Analysts are referencing the full sentence on account of reasons including Duggar's "prior sexual cheating of different minors" and "the amazing undertakings Duggar took to get and see kid sexual abuse materials (CSAM), the possibility of the CSAM he obtained and saw, his undertakings to camouflage his criminal lead, and his refusal to assume a sense of ownership with or perceive any of his law breaker direct."

What Sentence Is Josh Duggar's Legal Team Asking for?

In their undertakings to get Duggar a lighter sentence, his lawful guides battled that their client had never been charged or condemned for any infringement beforehand and that he get a sentence that is "satisfactory, but not more unmistakable than required." The update continued to examine, "Duggar demands that this Court recall him for the singular he is and the singular he can

Josh Duggar: His Drift

become," and sure-fire that he "will continue with a valuable and genuine presence following any sentence constrained by this Court."

The thing Has Anna Duggar Said About Josh Duggar's Sentencing?

Duggar's soul mate, Anna Duggar, introduced a letter to the court on March 11, saying that her better half is a respectable man and eminent father to a few's seven youths.

"He is a sort, valuing, consistent, and caring father and mate — his fundamental focus all through regular day to day existence. My adolescents and I rely upon Joshua for financial, up close and personal, and genuine assistance. Various others depend upon Joshua, also. Joshua is a man who routinely contributes his time, organizations, and resources, trying to add to our neighbourhood people in really bad shape," she wrote to Judge Timothy Brooks.

Anna added, "Joshua is surrounded by people who will encourage him to continue to transform into the best man, father, and business he can be. I ask that you consider re-joining us as a family again soon," but she said that she sorted out "the genuineness of this."

Hendrich Miller

What Letters Have the Duggar Family Mailed in?

Duggar's mom, Michelle Duggar, father-in-law Michael Keller and brother-in-law David Waller moreover made letters to the adjudicator attesting Josh's extraordinary individual and the sum he's needed in the presences of Anna and their children. A couple of Duggar's 18 family straightforwardly censured their family after his conviction.

CHAPTER 7

Josh Duggar Trial

Previous unscripted television star Josh Duggar was condemned Wednesday to 151 months in jail, over 12 years. Duggar, who was sentenced in December on government charges of getting and having youngster sexual entertainment, had looked as long as 20 years.

Examiners had looked for greatest sentence for Duggar, whose huge family was the focal point of TLC's "19 Kids and then some" unscripted TV drama. They contended in a pre-condemning court recording that Duggar has a "well established, unavoidable and brutal sexual interest in kids."

Duggar, whose legal counsellors looked for a five-year sentence, keeps up with his guiltlessness and has said he will pursue.

On Tuesday, U.S. Region Judge Timothy Brooks in Fayetteville, around 140 miles northwest of Little Rock, denied Duggar's solicitation for an exoneration or another preliminary.

Duggar was captured in April 2021 after a Little Rock police analyst found youngster pornography documents were being shared by a PC followed to Duggar. Examiners affirmed that pictures portraying the sexual maltreatment of youngsters, including little children, were downloaded in 2019 onto a PC at a vehicle sales centre Duggar possessed.

Tender loving care dropped "19 Kids and then some" in 2015 following claims that Duggar had attacked four of his sisters and a sitter years sooner. Specialists started researching the maltreatment in 2006 subsequent to getting a tip from a family companion however reasoned that the legal time limit on any potential charges had lapsed

Duggar's folks said he had admitted to the caressing and apologized. After the charges remerged in 2015, Duggar apologized openly for unknown way of behaving and surrendered as a lobbyist for the Family Research Council, a moderate Christian gathering.

Months after the fact, he openly apologized for betraying his better half and a porn habit, for which he then looked for treatment.

In looking for a 20-year sentence, examiners referred to the realistic pictures - and the times of the youngsters in question - as well as court declaration about the supposed maltreatment of Duggar's sisters.

Duggar's previous way of behaving "gives a disturbing window into the degree of his sexual interest in youngsters that the Court ought to consider at condemning," government examiners wrote in their condemning reminder.

CONCLUSION

"This previous direct, when seen close by the lead for which he has been sentenced, clarifies that Duggar has a firmly established, unavoidable, and brutal sexual interest in youngsters, and a readiness to follow up on that interest" the court documenting said.

Examiners likewise noticed that Duggar's PC had been apportioned to sidestep responsibility programming that had been introduced to answer to his significant other movement, for example, pornography look, authorities on the matter agree.

"There is basically no sign that Duggar will anytime take the steps essential to change this illustration of lead and address his inclination for minor females," analysts created.

Duggar has kept up with that he's guiltless and that he plans to pursue, his lawyers wrote in their condemning notice.

"Duggar acknowledges that he is under the steady gaze of this Court for condemning and that this Court should force a punishment," his lawyers composed. "That is equity. However, Duggar likewise requests to this Court's carefulness to treat that equity with leniency."

Made in the USA
Monee, IL
22 February 2023

28454632R00037